101 Facts About

PETS

101 Facts About

101 FACTS ABOUT

FERRETS

Published by Ringpress Books Limited,
PO Box 8, Lydney, Gloucestershire,
GL15 4YN, United Kingdom.

Design: Sara Howell

First Published 2001
© 2001 RINGPRESS BOOKS LIMITED

ISBN 1 86054 216 6

Printed in Hong Kong through Printworks Int. Ltd

0 9 8 7 6 5 4 3 2 1

101 FACTS ABOUT

FERRETS

Claire Horton-Bussey

Ringpress Books

1 Ferrets are **domestic** animals (tame pets), that have lived with humans for thousands of years.

2 The Romans used ferrets as far back as 300 BC to hunt pests, such as rats, and to help get rabbits for people to eat.

3 They introduced the ferrets to Europe, and then European travellers took them to America.

4 Ferrets have also been used to carry cables through tunnels or pipes, in places too small for people to do these jobs.

5 To help themselves squeeze through small gaps, ferrets have developed very flexible ribs so they can flatten themselves and crawl into the tiniest of spaces.

Pet ferrets descend from the polecat.

8 Ferrets can live up to 15 years or more, although most live to around six to eight years.

6 Ferrets are not **rodents**. They are closer to cats and dogs than they are to mice or rats.

7 Ferrets belong to a group of animals called **mustalids**. Other animals in this group include polecats, otters, weasels and skunk.

5

9 Male ferrets are called **hobs**, and female ferrets are called **jills**. Hobs are usually larger than jills, and their heads may be a little wider.

10 When she is six months old, a jill will need to have an operation, to stop her being able to have any babies. It is important she has this done, as otherwise she can become very ill and may even die.

11 A hob can also have the operation, so he can't become a dad. The operation will also stop him smelling so strongly.

12 A group of ferrets is called a 'business of ferrets'. This is probably because ferrets are so active and busy.

15 Ferrets love human company, and enjoy playing lots of games – they won't be happy to stay in a cage all day on their own.

13 When someone is busy looking for something, you say they are 'ferreting' it out. This phrase comes from the ferret's natural hunting behaviour.

16 Tunnelling is a favourite game, and your ferret may try to dig through your carpet, or your sofa, especially if he isn't kept occupied with lots of games.

14 The word 'ferret' comes from the Latin word 'furo', meaning 'thief'. This is because the ferret is very good at taking things and hiding them!

17 If you would like a ferret, you will have to ask your vet if you are allowed one where you live, as some places in America do not allow people to keep them.

18 In some other towns or cities, you need special permission before you can buy a ferret.

19 Next, you will need to find a breeder – this is someone who has baby ferrets for sale.

20 A baby ferret is called a **kit**, and a group of kits is called a **litter**.

21 A jill will be pregnant for between 40 and 44 days, and then will give birth to the litter.

22 The average litter (pictured left) contains between six and eight ferrets, and a jill can have up to four litters a year, though this would be very bad for her health.

25 At 10 days of age, the kit's milk teeth will come through, and his canines (the long, sharp teeth at the sides of his mouth) will grow through after about six weeks.

23 When a kit is first born, he will not be able to see or hear. He will have no fur on his body, so he will rely on his mother, brothers and sisters to keep him warm.

26 A kit can leave his litter for his new home when he is between 10 and 12 weeks old.

24 After about five days, the kit's fur will start to grow through (pictured above), and his ears and eyes will start working after about three weeks.

27 The kits should all look healthy and lively. Their coats should be clean and in good condition, their eyes should look bright, and their ears and noses should be clean.

28 You should ask the breeder to handle the kits. If the ferrets are nervous or aggressive, they may not be used to very much human contact, and it is best to find another litter – one that likes people, rather than fears them.

29 Ferrets come in all types of colours, and when you pick your kit, you will have to decide which one you like best.

30 An **albino** ferret (pictured above) is white with red eyes. He shouldn't be confused with an ordinary white ferret that has darker eyes.

31 A **sable** ferret (pictured below) is a dark brown colour, with a lighter undercoat and darker feet.

32 A ferret can also have a coat that is the same colour as chocolate, though his undercoat will be a lighter shade.

33 A **cinnamon** ferret (pictured above) will have a red-brown coat, with darker legs.

34 **Siamese** is the word used for a ferret that has a lighter-coloured body than his legs and tail.

11

37 When a ferret has '**mitts**' it looks as if he is wearing little socks on his feet. '**Stockings**' look as if he is wearing longer socks, which reach further up his leg.

35 There are lots of coat patterns, too. A **dalmatian** ferret will have spots on his white coat, just as a Dalmatian dog has.

36 A ferret **mask** (pictured above) is where the face is coloured in such a way that it looks as if the animal is wearing a mask.

38 A '**blaze**' is when there is white on the forehead and down the neck.

39 A '**bib**' (pictured top right) is when there is white on the chest – just as if the ferret is wearing a baby's bib.

summer. This is because ferrets have more undercoat when it is colder, and their undercoat is a lighter colour than the topcoat.

40 As ferrets get older, their coat colour gets lighter. Very old ferrets can get grey or white hair — just as humans do!

41 A ferret's coat colour can also look paler in the winter than in the

42 Because ferrets can get bored easily, you might want to think about getting two kits instead of one. That way, they can play with each other when you are not able to be with them.

43 Some ferrets are kept outdoors, but it is best if pet ferrets live indoors, so that they don't become bored and unhappy. An indoor ferret will have much more contact with people, and will be much more confident.

44 Before you bring a ferret home, make sure your house is safe.

Check that there are no holes he can escape through, and no plants or wires that he can chew.

45 If you have small pets, like mice, hamsters, or gerbils, keep them out of reach, in a room where your ferret won't be allowed. Make sure the door is always shut so your ferret can't sneak in.

46 Ferrets usually get on well with dogs and cats, and they often become playmates. But you

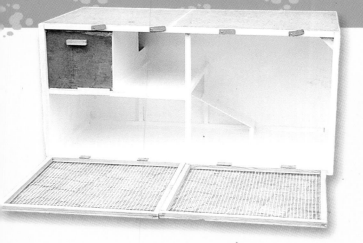

must never leave them alone together, and should introduce them carefully when they first meet, so they gradually get used to each other.

47 Your ferret must have somewhere to sleep. He will need a big cage (pictured above), somewhere it is safe for him to stay when you can't look after him (for example, at night).

48 He should never be kept in the cage for long periods throughout the day or he will become very unhappy. At the very least, your ferret should have two hours outside his cage every day.

49 Inside the cage, there should be shredded paper on the floor, and a little nestbox with a towel inside for bedding, where your ferret can curl up to sleep.

50 The cage should be strong and sturdy so your ferret cannot escape. A wooden frame with a wire-mesh front is ideal.

51 Always make sure the cage door is closed when he is inside, and ensure he can't tunnel out of the bottom of the cage by buying one that has a solid floor.

52 Put the cage out of direct sunlight and chilly draughts, so that your ferret doesn't get too hot or too cold.

53 Fresh water should be provided every day in a water bottle. A food bowl will also be needed; make sure it is heavy so your ferret can't tip it over.

Food bowl

Nesting material

Toy to play with

Litter tray

food from your pet shop (pictured below), or, if you can't find any, your pet can be given good-quality dry cat or kitten food.

56 His food dish should be cleaned every day, and he should always be able to get to his water bottle.

54 Your ferret should be fed little meals throughout the day. Three small meals is much better than giving him one big meal.

55 Ferrets are **carnivores**, which means they need to eat meat. You can buy special dry ferret

57 The instructions on the pack of food will tell you how much to feed. But all ferrets are different and you will need to work out how much to give, depending on your ferret's appetite.

58 Never let your ferret get over-weight, though, as it will be very bad for his health. You should always be able to feel his ribs along his chest, but he shouldn't look skinny.

59 As an occasional treat, you can feed your ferret a raw egg – he will love it! But don't feed eggs too much (more than once a week at the most) or he may become bald. Do not feed your ferrets chocolate or sweet cookies.

60 An indoor ferret can be house-trained. Fill a litter tray with about 1½ inches (4 cms) of cat litter, and place it in a corner of the room your ferret is in.

61 Put your ferret in his littertray when he first wakes up, after he has

had a play, and after he has eaten. These are the times when ferrets usually need to go to the toilet.

62 Ask an adult to empty the ferret's littertray every day, as ferrets are very clean animals and do not like using dirty trays.

63 When your ferret uses his tray for the first few times, he should be given a tasty treat to show him that he has been very good.

65 Handle your ferret firmly but gently. When you pick him up (pictured left), put your hand over his shoulders, so your fingers are around the front of his chest. Then support his lower body with your other hand. He should be very comfortable in this position.

66 Never pick him up when he is half asleep, as he may nip you out of fear. Ferrets sleep very deeply (pictured top right) – and sometimes it takes them several minutes to come round.

64 Your ferret should be handled a lot while he is a kit, so that he grows up not to fear humans. Make sure an adult is available to help you.

69 Teach your ferret to come by calling his name and showing him a tasty treat. He will soon learn that when you call him, he should come straight away!

67 Kits tend to be a little nippy, so they need to be taught that nipping is not allowed.

68 If your ferret nips you, you should say "No" very firmly, and then ignore him. That way, he learns that nipping is wrong, and that it is not a game.

72 At first, just get your ferret used to wearing his harness. When he is happy wearing it, attach the lead (pictured below).

73 Take a few steps forward and call his name, offering a treat, so he follows you.

70 You can also train your ferret to walk on a lead. You can buy a harness (pictured above) which fits over your ferret's body.

71 Practise lead-training indoors. Make sure your ferret is fully vaccinated before venturing outside.

76 Ferrets are very lively animals and will need play sessions with you several times a day.

77 A rope tug-toy will give hours of fun, as will pvc tubes, golf balls and cardboard tubes.

74 By holding a treat, you can train your ferret to follow your hand over a small box, or even through a hoop.

75 Or you could hold a treat up high, so your ferret has to stand on his back legs to reach it.

80 In nice weather, your ferret can play in an outdoor run. Make sure it has a solid bottom, so your pet can't escape.

81 Always put the run in the shade, and the water bottle should also be transferred.

78 Try hiding from your ferret and calling his name. When he finds you, give him a treat.

79 Create a maze of tunnels for your ferret out of sturdy boxes, or perhaps let him play in an old pillowcase or sleeping bag – he'll love it!

82 Like the skunk and the polecat, ferrets have a distinct smell. Ferrets

release more smell when they feel threatened.

83 They also use their scent to tell other animals to keep away from their territory.

84 To make sure your ferret doesn't smell horrible, his bedding should be replaced every day.

85 Ferrets have a very thick coat, made up of a topcoat, which is waterproof, and a softer undercoat which keeps them warm.

86 Use a medium-soft bristle brush to groom your ferret. Then comb him (pictured below) to remove any tangles.

87 Ferrets will moult – or lose – their coat twice a year. This happens in spring and in autumn/fall. A new coat will soon grow back.

88 If you bath your ferret too much, he will make up for losing the natural oils in his coat by becoming oilier – and smellier – than before! A bath every couple of months is fine.

89 Ferrets can get fleas, and, if this happens, you can bath him using a kitten-safe flea shampoo. Rinse the coat thoroughly, and then dry your ferret with a towel.

90 If your ferret's nails do not wear down naturally, you may need to have them cut. Your vet will do this for you.

91 Feeding your ferret hard, dry food should keep his teeth clean (pictured below), but if his teeth need cleaning, ask your vet to help.

92 Check your ferret's ears to make sure they are clean and smell

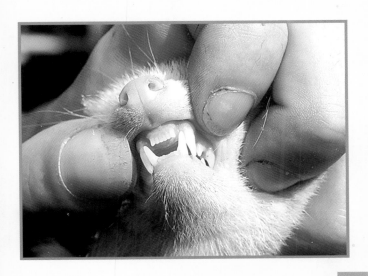

fresh. If they smell foul and have a dark-grey wax, your ferret may have ear mites. Consult your vet.

93 Take your ferret to the vet every year, so he can have any booster vaccinations and a general check-up.

95 If they are very frightened or are in pain, they will scream.

96 Like cats, ferrets will hiss when they are fighting. They do this to warn the other ferret that they are very cross and to make him go away.

94 Ferrets make lots of interesting noises. They will whine if they are excited, or make a giggling, chuckling sound if they are having fun.

97 Also like cats, a ferret can fluff up his tail to make it look big and menacing.

100 If your ferret sneezes, he may have a cold. Always talk to your vet, if you think your ferret is unwell.

101 As long as you look after your ferret properly, he will give you lots of love and fun for many years to come.

98 A ferret can also make his hair stand on end to make the other animal think he is bigger and stronger than he actually is.

99 If your ferret is nervous or excited, you may see him shiver.

GLOSSARY

Albino: a white ferret with red eyes.

Bib: a white marking on a ferret's chest.

Blaze: a white marking on the forehead and down the neck.

Carnivore: a meat-eater.

Cinnamon: a red-brown ferret with darker legs.

Dalmatian: a white ferret with dark spots on his coat.

Domestic: tame, not wild.

Hob: a male ferret.

Jill: a female ferret.

Kit: a baby ferret.

Litter: a group of kits.

Mask: where the face is coloured so that it looks as if the ferret is wearing a mask.

Mitts: when the ferret's feet are a different colour to his legs, so it looks as if he is wearing little socks.

Mustalids: a group of animals, that includes the ferret, polecat, otter, weasel, and skunk.

Rodents: a group of animals that gnaw, which includes the hamster, rat, mouse and gerbil.

Sable: a dark brown ferret with a lighter undercoat and darker feet.

Siamese: a ferret with a lighter body than his legs and tail.

Stockings: these are like mitts, but reach further up the ferret's leg, so that it looks as if he is wearing long socks.

MORE BOOKS TO READ

All About Your Ferret
Sheila Crompton
(Ringpress Books)

Pet Owner's Guide to the Ferret
Dennis Kelsey-Wood
(Ringpress Books)

My Pet Ferrets
Amy Gelman and Andy King
(Lerner Publishing Group)

Your First Ferret
Adelle Porch
(TFH Publications)

 # WEBSITES

Ferret care
www.ferretnook.com/ferretcare.html

Ferret net
www.ferret.net/

Ferret organisation
www.oregon-ferret.org/
articles/fpet.html

Treasured ferrets
www.umuc.edu/~pball

To find additional websites, use a reliable search engine to find one or more of the following key words: **ferret**, **ferret care**, **pet ferrets**.

INDEX